# Palmetto & Palash

Richi Aria

Presentation by *BookLeaf Publishing*

Web: www.bookleafpub.com

E-mail: info@bookleafpub.com

ISBN: 9789363311466

First edition 2024

# Following

Marveling the sky beyond the traveling glass, childhood naivete had convinced me that the sun had been accompanying me wherever I went.

Through the drives from school to home to the doctors to the shop and back to school again with the coming morning, the Sun had been my focus in those moments in between, moments between the necessary that necessitated only my focus- for as long as I had focused, the sun had followed.

Yet as guiding asphalt became weathered and hope meandered, adolescent cynicism had convinced me to force a shadow over my eyes to shield from the sun's painful brightness.

When the thick cloak of mature skepticism had grown heavy, it was undeniable that nothing could stop the sun's light from reaching me, from seeping through the pores of the fabric that wrapped me in stagnation.

Welcoming the sun again was not enough, for I had to welcome my own movement. I had to

welcome confusion, frustration, and fear, fear of
losing the light in light of looking for it.

What a futile fear that was,

To welcome the sun is to say that no matter
which direction I move, by focusing on the light,
I invite it to follow me!

# Turning

Why even try? That was the pervasive mantra that had slithered its way into every decision, every intention, each interaction and every dream. With each repetition, I spindled a new thread around my body until I had been completely enclosed in a cocoon of comfortable paranoia.

I rested, exhausted from fleeing a threat I had persuaded myself was real.

Woven withdrawal strayed me away from the risk of showing my true face, or any face at all. I was disillusioned by the comfort I had created, thinking it infinitely preferable to my perceived inevitability of failure.

It was comfortable to believe that I had seen everything I needed to see, It was comfortable to believe that I had met everyone I needed to meet, It was comfortable to believe that I had felt everything I needed to feel.

But to be comfortable is not to be fulfilled. When did I replace trying with assuming? When

would I untap the potential that I had left
dormant and dusty for far too long? When would
my metamorphosis finally take shape?

Thread by thread, I unraveled my cocoon
through new thoughts, new actions. There was
more to see, more to meet, more to feel. The
breeze brushing by my wings was fresh, a
sensation that took me by surprise as I stepped
into this nature.

Finally, there was more to do and more to be.

For the monotony of being surrounded by stones
disappears once I work to leave none of them
unturned!

# Interlude - The Real World

"The Real World" was paraded to me
as competition, criticism, and callousness
of flaunting, taunting, and daunting.

Pastors of paradox, they see
their self-fulfilling prophecies
and fear as necessity

But you, you are free
to see the beauty
they've forgotten.

# Chasing

I had received a message from my mother late last night, she had asked me if I had seen the full moon that was to adorn the sky at that hour.

A pursuer of luminosity, my ardor immediately pulled my weary body away from my bed and into the outside. Despite a paralleling force that pulled my eyelids down, my footsteps wandered frantically in search of the full moon.

Yet all I could see were trees and lights and buildings that had all conspired to obscure my view.

A pursuer of ambition, my avoidance of abandonment carried my pattering strides to the highest point to which I could climb. I ventured higher than the trees, higher than the lights, higher than the buildings.

And yet, the sky only bored into me with its empty sapphire expanse.

As the beat of my heart slowed and the weight of unmet expectation pressed against my chest, I embarked on the feeble trudge of my return. Had I not climbed high enough? Had I been too late? Was seeing the full moon simply not in my fate?

Drowsiness catching up to me, I paused at an ordinary square in the sidewalk. A deep breath overtook me, my head naturally tilting back. And in an instant- there the full moon was, hanging low in the sky and beaming down at me with a forgiving, majestic glow. From the humblest angle, I was gifted with the grandest sight.

I stood awestruck, an inquisitive smile was donning my face as the truth was dawning on me: How foolish I could be, to overlook the horizon in pursuit of the summit- for the moon does not hide; it was my perspective that had blinded me.

Greatness will reveal itself when I not only chase what is above but appreciate what is around!

# Waiting

Locked inside a motionless car, I find myself adrift in the sea of waiting. The reason for our pause has long since faded from memory, but the image of the clouds above remain etched in my mind's eye. They hung suspended, ornaments in a vast canvas of blue, their stillness a glaring reminder of my own.

My concentration, at first fixed on the celestial tableau, gradually turns inward. The landscape of my thoughts shifts and morphs, meandering through the valleys of temporary sorrows and scaling the peaks of momentary fascinations. Time becomes fluid, its passage unmarked and unnoticed.

When at last I resurface from the depths of my reverie, I'm startled to find the world has moved on without me. The sky that greets me is a stranger - new clouds have taken up residence, their shapes and patterns unfamiliar yet intriguing.

A pang of regret washes over me. How I wish I had been more present, more attentive to the

subtle ballet playing out right in front of me. If
only I had lifted my eyes more often, I might
have witnessed the gradual metamorphosis of
the heavens. I could have seen the old clouds
slowly dissipating, watched as new formations
took shape, observed the constant ebb and flow
of atmospheric artistry.

As I sit there, contemplating the new view
before me, I set a goal- from now on, I'll strive
to be more aware, to lift my gaze more often
from the confines of my inner world.

For in those small moments of attention, in those
brief glances upward, is the potential to witness
the subtle magic of change as it unfolds!

# Separating

Passing through the heart of my university campus, I take in the sight of fallen petals that have come together to kindly decorate the pond with their vibrant hues. Each one a fragment of a flower that was lovingly nurtured by the sun's warmth and the Earth's embrace, these oblivious castaways find themselves in an unfamiliar realm.

Some petals will float effortlessly, skimming the surface with delicate grace. They will be whisked away towards the distant shore, where new landscapes will await them and they will one day fade into the soil. However, others will waver in their buoyancy, sinking slowly beneath the pond's tranquil facade, resting upon the sediment where light will fade alongside them.

No aspect of this odyssey was based in their choice. Each petal had been torn away by forces beyond their control- a gust of wind, a sudden downpour, a pesky pest. Regardless, each petal mirroring the students I had been seeing similarly scattered about, was now part of a larger story, a narrative written by the elements that shaped its path. No matter where they would go, they would never attach to the stem that birthed them in the way they once had been.

This separation was not an end but a continuation, a new chapter in the story of existence. It is in this departure that I find myself part of the perpetual cycle of life- where growth yields to decay and decay yields to growth, and each phase is essential for renewal.

My life's journey is not merely about remaining rooted, but about embracing those inevitable transitions and transformations that do nothing less than shape my existence. In this cycle of rot and vitality, in nature's perpetual dance of departure and return, is the essence of my being-

It's not the leaving that defines me, but the growth I nurture in my wake!

# Interlude - Origami

We begin with a simple blank square
overflowing with potential,

Patiently waiting for the creases of life
and the movements of decisions
to make something beautiful of ourselves

What have you folded into?
A complex creation,
or a simple truth?

Perhaps the beauty is found
not in the final form,
but in the courage to transform!

# Searching

Years ago, my teacher scrawled at the whiteboard and announced to us Newton's laws of motion. Entranced in my sedentary slumber, I had yet to understand the broader application these relationships of objects and forces would have.

For since the dawn of intelligent primate minds, there has been wonder about a life beyond this- beyond Earth, beyond humans. As technology budded and bloomed, what was once wonder turned into a search. A search that has transcended time, a motion that can only be stopped by the force of the find.

Yet despite eons of possibility to find or be found… nothing. The only signs in space are the ones we create, etched into gold for only us.

We have been eternally educated on our isolation- our one humanity, our one life. Why, with such scarcity, does humanity squander our single chance with cruelty, with every being both a target and arrow, how do we treat our one shot with such careless aim?

These times of cruelty are captivating, holding our minds hostage into forgetting both the presence and value of kindness. While momentous cruelty seems infinitely more memorable, mundane kindness can hold the same momentum. I hold the power to choose which cycles I continue- and I owe it to those who were kind to me that I am kind to others. No matter the size of their sacrifice, my respect comes in emulation.

To be giving is to defy an order that denies our nature as human beings.

I will not let the inertia of kindness end with me!

# Setting

Leaning against the fence at the precipice of the balcony, my eyes are fixed on the horizon where the sun dips below the skyline. The day's last light paints the clouds in hues of amber and rose, a masterpiece that will soon fade into the night's embrace.

My mind wanders to the countless sunsets I've witnessed, each one a gift I've often taken for granted. How many times have I rushed through my days, barely glancing at the sky, too consumed by the relentless march of time and the weight of my ambitions?

My gratitude should not be a caveat or an afterthought. It's not a comparison to others' misfortunes or a deflection from my own struggles. No, gratitude is a lens through which I can view my world anew, transforming the prosaic into the profound.

I think of the mornings I've cursed, the routines that felt like shackles. Yet now, in retrospect, these very moments shimmer with a confusing nostalgia. The experiences were bitter, yes, but those memories taste sweet.

How strange it is that I often hated the days but loved the memories they created. I sought happiness in an impossible, nebulous future, always chasing, never quite grasping. But here, in this moment, I find profound joy in the tangible present - the cool breeze on my skin, the fading warmth of the sun, the steady rhythm of my breath.

I've saved my gratitude for grand experiences, for milestones and achievements. But what of the default state of my existence? The miracle of waking each morning, of having a place to call home, of the countless invisible threads that weave the tapestry of my daily life?

Being grateful only in hindsight is a tragedy of the human condition. We truly realize what we have only when it's gone, like water slipping through our fingers. But what if gratitude could be perpetual, a constant undercurrent in the river of our consciousness?

As the last sliver of sun disappears and the first stars begin to twinkle, I silently vow: I will not wait for loss to appreciate what I have. I will not defer my happiness to some distant future. Instead, I will cultivate gratitude in every breath, finding wonder in the ordinary and joy in the journey.

For in this moment, standing between day and night, past and future, I am alive. And that, in itself, is worthy of infinite gratitude!

# Deciding

The passenger seat of my friend's car treated me lovingly as I dozed, lethargically watching the trees pass by in the twilight. Serendipitously, my friend calls my dampened attention to a streak of bluish light blazing across the darkness- a shooting star. Startled with awe, My lips move in silent supplication, as if my desires could ride that fleeting tail of celestial dust to fruition.

The memory of childhood birthdays floods my senses - the warm glow of candles atop a frosted cake, their flames shivering with anticipation. I recall the weight of wishes held in a single breath, waiting to be released in a simple gust. As wax melted and smoke curled upwards, I could believe my dreams were ascending, carried on wisps to some higher power that could make them real.

Then, I find myself pausing by a fountain in a bustling square. The water's surface shimmers with countless coins, each one a metallic prayer tossed by hopeful hands. I fish a coin from my wallet, its cold weight a reminder of the exchange about to be made. With a flick of my wrist, it arcs through the air, breaking the water's surface with a soft noise. As its ripples spread outward, I ponder the cumulative weight of all these submerged wishes.

These acts - wishing on stars, blowing out candles, tossing coins - they all require a form of sacrifice. The star's brilliance fades, the candle's flame is extinguished, the coin is relinquished. To wish is to give something up, to acknowledge that I cannot have it all, as much as I might try.

I think of all the wishes I've made, the dreams I've chased, the hopes I've nurtured. Each one has come at a cost - time, energy, opportunities forsaken for others pursued. The universe, in its infinite wisdom, seems to operate on a principle of exchange. For every path chosen, others must be left unexplored. It's a delicate balance between what I yearn for and what I am willing to give up.

The truest magic lies not in the fulfillment of my wishes, but in the growth that comes from making them - in learning to choose wisely, to sacrifice gracefully, and to find contentment in the imperfect beauty of my limited, yet wonderfully rich, human experience!

# Interlude - Jack Of All Trades

Scattered seeds
in many fields
or a single tree
deeply rooted?

Which bears more fruit?
The experimental mind, or the focused soul?

The answer should be considered
not in choosing, but in growing
wherever we're planted!

# Bursting

The evening erupts in a symphony of light and sound, each firework an ephemeral star born and dying in the span of a breath. Eyes wide to capture each moment of brilliance, each burst feels like a sparkling nebula blooming impossibly close, as if the cosmos themself were descending on me.

In my awe, a familiar whisper of guilt lays its heavy hand on my shoulder. My mind, ever the diligent archivist, begins to catalog the myriad ways these dazzling displays bring pain to others. The triggering betrayal of the very veterans this holiday is supposed to commemorate, the thousands of people who are living their last seconds with all ten fingers, down to the very air we breathe being tainted by the smoke and chemicals released by this spectacle.

Yet tonight, I make a choice. I gently push aside these thoughts, not dismissing them entirely, but allowing them to rest at the edges of my consciousness. For once, I permit myself the luxury of unadulterated joy. I embrace the childlike wonder that bubbles up within me, marveling at each burst of color as if I had never seen color before.

Is it selfish to focus solely on my own happiness in this moment? Perhaps. But my appreciation of this beautiful display does not diminish the struggles of others, nor does it negate the very real concerns that exist. The sky bears witness to our celebrations and our sorrows alike; It judges neither.

As the grand finale turns night into day for one last glorious instant, I feel the corners of my lips tug upwards into a smile. In this moment, I am only happy.

And I am allowed to feel joy regardless of caveats!

# Tilting

My favorite planet is Neptune. While it may not have the speed of Mercury, the beauty of Venus, the color of Mars, the size of Jupiter, the rings of Saturn, the name of Uranus, or the controversy of Pluto, Neptune is special in its peculiar rotation, a cosmic oddity in our solar system.

With its wide and retrograde spin, it rings of how the concept of "strange" is merely a construct of the majority. Neptune twirls to its own rhythm, unbothered by the conformity of its celestial neighbors.

What defines our norm? Is it not just a silent and collective agreement, a shared illusion? On Earth, people scramble and scheme for diamonds, their infrequency driving their value to dizzying heights. Yet on Neptune, these precious gems rain from above in a surreal downpour of crystallized carbon.

What palpable irony- how one of our most coveted treasures exists in cosmic abundance, yet remains out of reach. The rarity that makes diamonds valuable on Earth is rendered meaningless in the vast expanse of the Universe.

Value is not intrinsic but assigned. It's a human invention, a shared story we tell ourselves to make sense of our world and our place in it. The diamond that adorns a ring, symbol of eternal love and commitment, holds no more inherent worth than the pebbles beneath my feet. Its value lies not in its molecular structure, but in the meaning we imbue it with.

My perceptions, my values, my very definition of normalcy- all are as fluid and changeable as the methane clouds swirling in Neptune's atmosphere. What I deem odd or precious right now is simply a reflection of a limited perspective, a tiny fragment of the infinite cosmic quilt.

I find my place not by conforming but by truly choosing!

# Reflecting

I stand before the mirror, observing my face. These eyes, windows to a soul that has witnessed both too much and too little. They've seen heartache and joy, disappointment and triumph, yet they hunger for more experiences, more understanding. The paradox of being both world-weary and naive simultaneously etches itself in the creases around my eyes.

My focus shifts to my nose, a feature that has borne the brunt of shame and ridicule. Its shape, a testament to my heritage, has been a target for those who throw disgust on difference. Yet, as I trace its contours with my eyes, I see the strength of generations, the resilience of a lineage that refused to be erased.

My lips shift slightly, and I'm reminded of all the times my mouth has betrayed me, words tumbling out in the wrong order, at the wrong time. How often have I cursed this mouth for its missteps, for the relationships strained by its clumsiness? Despite it all, gratitude washes over me. For every misspoken word, there was an attempt at connection, at truth. This mouth, imperfect as it may be, keeps trying, keeps reaching out.

I may not love myself, not yet. But in this moment, I promise: I will at least support myself.

No, I may not be the best or the smartest in any conventional sense. But I am the best version of myself that I can be right now. I am the smartest in the unique way my mind works, in the connections only I can make. And even as I acknowledge that others may surpass me in various ways, I still feel a surge of pride and determination.

As I step back from the mirror, a small smile plays on my lips. I realize that I am worthy of my own applause. Not because I've achieved greatness by anyone else's standards, but because I continue to show up, to try, to grow.

After everything, I'm still rooting for me!

# Interlude - Intersections

Interlude - Intersections

The curse of being different is to either
be denied deserved attention
or bombarded with the wrong kind

But the blessing
is being me, and being true

A Mandala of infinite details,
my wholeness is not negotiable.

For in a world of Either/Or,
I will always dare to be And.

# Feeding

A shaky sigh escapes me, hands clutching at my knees with my head bowing down amidst an active shift in the outside's oppressive heat. Suddenly, my tedium is halted by a searing prickle flaring around my ankles. Bug bites.

Reverberating throughout my body, the instinct to tear at my skin is screaming at me. The allure of the infinite loop of the itch and the scratch calls to me, the desperation to feed my brain's desire for serotonin, and to keep on keep on keep on feeding it violently fights with my rationality. Reason reminds me that to scratch would mean breaking down my loyal skin- or more importantly, amplifying the swell of the bug bites' bumps. It will heal soon. It will heal soon, it will heal soon.

Taking all my resistance, I methodically navigate my hands away from where they so badly want to be, straying my mind away from the temptation of immediate relief that would only cause myself prolonged harm. Each second is slow and maddening.

But gradually, madness succumbs to relief. The sting subsides, the swelling smooths, and the urge to commit such an act of sabotage onto myself dissolves. The irritation eventually becomes nothing but a distant memory, and I thank myself for practicing such patience.

My path to enduring peace often lies in enduring the momentary pain of restraint, for healing awaits on the other side!

# Devouring

I stood in my kitchen, meticulously peeling back the last of the pith of an orange that rested in my hand. At long last, I could bring the segment to my teeth, and allow the invigorating flood of sweetness to awaken my senses. I savor the tender touch of the orange's flesh upon my tongue, celebrating a ritual of nature's artistry.

As I proceed to devour every last piece, citrusy juice dripping down my fingers, I am connected to the lineage of hands that have touched this orange- directly and indirectly.

From the workers who picked the ripe fruit under a generously blazing sun, to the growers who carefully tended to the trees, to the inventors of the machinery that was utilized throughout, to the first Mesopotamian woman who discovered that nurturing a seed from the soil would ultimately help nurture our bodies- from all their mothers, fathers, friends, and everything in their worlds that brought them to those points.

While I stand in this room, every wall and
window, every tile under my feet, is a symbol of
human endeavor and continuity- people who
gave their time, their labor, their ingenuity, each
leaving an indelible mark on the world.

The range across my hands is a testament of
their toil, just as the space I occupy is a mosaic
of human achievement. Absolutely nothing that I
have ever seen or touched has been untouched
by human contribution, by the convergence of
billions of cumulative memories. For all of this,
I am grateful.

For it takes one to experience a moment but
millions to make it!

# Drifting

I wasn't sure how much more I could take. Whether it was old problems mockingly resurfacing or new problems boisterously emerging, one thing would be sure: they would grow bigger, and bigger, and bigger.

I wasn't sure how much more I could walk. The constant and easy motion was the perfect escape from my troubles, for the colors of the sky never failed to enamor me. Indefinite walks into the sunset always evoked tranquility until it was time to return back through the possibly perilous dark.

Amidst my hurried amble, temptation overpowered my anxieties and I stood still to look up at the stars. As I gazed, it befell me how there is no end to the above. That for every second I am existing, the universe is expanding- and I am becoming smaller, and smaller, and smaller.

Now I understand why time goes faster as time goes on.

Everything I know is getting closer, being
pushed together by the increasing surrounds of
space. As if the universe itself is paradoxically
drawing my world inward, pulling all its
elements into a tighter embrace. This is the
cosmic compression that makes my years more
fleeting and my days more formidable.

Enveloped in eternity, my feelings are difficult
to discern. The scarcity of my world makes it
more valuable, but the specificity of my
problems makes them more piercing.

Yet the shine of the stars, with their light that has
traveled unfathomable distances through the
dark to reach my eyes, fills me with belief that
my endurance will lead me to the right eyes as
well.

Because while the universe is vast and
ever-changing, so am I!